The College Blue Book

Written and Compiled
by
Anthony J. D'Angelo

Arkad Press
Three Bridges, New Jersey

Published in the United States of America by Arkad Press
Printing by David Morton
Design and Typesetting by Sallie Carr & Deborah Jo Angus
Edited by Bernice Lauterbach & Phil Tripp
Library of Congress Cataloging-in Publication Data
D'Angelo, Anthony J., 1972-
The College Blue Book
1. Quotations, thoughts, maxims 2. College, student life
3. Personal Development & Education 4. Self-Reliance 5. Humanitarianism
Library of Congress Catalog Card Number: 95-90377
ISBN 0-9646957-0-7 (paperback)

BOOKS ARE AVAILABLE AT QUANTITY DISCOUNTS WHEN USED FOR
FRESHMAN ORIENTATION, COMMENCEMENT GIFTS OR ANYTHING ELSE THAT
ENCOURAGES YOUNG PEOPLE TO MAKE THIS WORLD A BETTER PLACE.
FOR MORE INFORMATION PLEASE CALL THE COLLEGE BLUE BOOK ORDER CENTER
AT (609) 397-5600 OR E-MAIL YOUR REQUEST TO: info@empowerx.org. THANK YOU.

This book is printed on recycled paper.

Don't mess with mother nature.

RECYCLE! REDUCE! REUSE!

This book is dedicated to the young people of this world.
For without you, our lives would have but little meaning.

100% of the proceeds generated from this book, go directly
back to helping EmPower X! empower young people.

A Sincere Thanks

This book would not be possible if it were not for the generous support of the following individuals: Dr. Madeline Wing Adler, Dr. Fred Lane, Dr. Paul Oliaro, Dr. Stan Yarosewick, Joe Hamel, Kevin Garvey, Mr. John Unruh, Bernie Carrozza, Martha Carson-Gentry, Johanna Havilick, Bill Hughes, Dr. Jim McCormick, Mr. Fitz Dixon, the ENTIRE division of Student Affairs at West Chester University, especially Steve Mckerinan, Phil Tripp, Matt Bricketto, Charlie Warner, Diane DeVestern, Dave Timmann, Pete Galloway, Tom Purce, Mel Joesphs, Sueanne Robbins, Steve Gambino, Jackie Hodes, Robin Garrett, Skip Hudson, Maggie Tripp, and Latona Williams. Every single teacher, counselor, secretary and staff member that I ever had the opportunity to learn from, especially Mr. Larry Hoerner, Father Dave Givey, Dr. Raymond Friday, Mr. Mike Roe, Mr. Tony Carrozza, Mr. Brian Cashman, Hanna Leigey, and Dr. Andrew Dinnimann. And all of the schools that I have ever attended, including West Chester University, Cedar Cliff High School, New Cumberland Middle School and Manor Elementary School. Special thanks to Bernie Lauterbach for proofreading and to former president Jimmy Carter for promoting world peace.

Also to all of my friends from both the "Cliff" and WCU, especially Paul "Yackie" Redclift, Justin "Bake" Murphy, Eric Grode, Shelley Rhodes, John & Tara Nelson, Donavan Murray, Todd Richman, Matt Campbell, Mark Brown, Matt Banko, Kathy Markel, Sulit, My OX brothers, the WCU SGA, Irv Hartman, Steve Murphy, Chris Snock, Teddy Rafeto, Chris "Mellon" Luongo, Andy Shoffner, Megan Brolly, Betsy Schmid, and many, many others.

To my most influential and inspiring mentors whom I have yet to meet- Anthony Robbins, Stephen Covey, Brian Tracy, Richard Bandler, John Grinder, Robert Diltz, Bill Gates, Denis Waitley, Alvin & Heidi Toffler, Michael Gerber, Paul Zane Pilzer, Jay Abraham, Tom Peters, Vic Conant, Wayne Huizenga, Roger & Rebecca Merrill, Harvey Mackay and Gerald Coffee. You each have given me a special gift which I intend to share with others. That gift is to constantly strive to make this big blue marble a better place for all of us.

The most sincere of thanks goes to no other than my families & VIPs. To my extended family who blessed me with good genes, good times and a positive out look on life. To my friend and associate, John Cornele, for his commitment to Integrity. To my friend Doc, thank you for all of his love, laughter and Buddhist's Delights. To my partner and wing man Chris Snock, for his unyielding commitment, support and passion to spread the EmPower X! message. To my second family in New Jersey—the Randazzese's—Sal, Fran, Lisa, Lamby, Phyllis, and Jim for all your support, love and good chili. And most of all, to the most precious people in my life. To my living heroes, my grandmothers, both of whom have taught me that "old" is a state of mind and "young" is a state of soul. To my best friend and soul mate, Chris "Snugs" Randazzese, who has given me the gift of Joy. To my sister, Tina, who has given me the gift of Courage. To my brother, Mike, who has given me the gift of Proactivism. To my father, Mike, who has given me the gift of Patience. And to my mother, Janet, who has given me the gift of Passion for life.

Thank you all, I am truly blessed.

FORWARD

Ah, our college years. Probably one of the most wondrous experiences that we'll ever have. A time of change, a time of independence, a time of laughter, a time of tears and, most of all, a time of unlimited growth.

As we learn from each passing moment of life, we are constantly being shaped and molded into the person we are becoming. During our college days, we have the great opportunity to become students of our own personal growth and development. Valuable lessons are taught to us by our families, our friends, our professors, our advisors and yes, even by our college's administrators. But even more valuable than the lessons being taught, are the ones that we learn through our own experiences.

I wrote <u>The College Blue Book</u>, to support our never ending search for the best within ourselves. Experience is not what happens to us, rather it is what we do with what happens to us. The goal of this book is to give you a different way to look at things. Some things might make you laugh, some might make you cry, but most of all, they will inspire you to reflect on this truly wondrous experience.

> *"Two roads diverged in a wood, and I –*
> *I took the one-less traveled by,*
> *And that has made all the difference."*

Robert Frost

I encourage you to not follow in someone else's footsteps. Rather, look deep within yourself and discover one of the greatest journeys — creating your own path. Enjoy the adventure!

Live life without regrets,
Tony D'Angelo

001. Get the name of your roommate and her hometown BEFORE you move, in August.

002. Go grocery shopping with your roommates at 2 a.m.; you'll avoid all the crowds and you'll have one hell of a time.

003. Become close friends with a person from another country.

004. Become close friends with a person who can type well.

005. Take Computers 101 your freshman year and retake it your last semester; no doubt the technology will change in that short bit of time.

006. Play "These Are Days" by 10,000 Maniacs on your stereo every morning before class and let it become your anthem.

007. Call your Mother.

008. Write to your Father.

009. Drink two big glasses of water before going to bed following a big night of partying.

010. Remember who you are and where you are from.

011. Dream of where you are going and who you are becoming.

012. Save your flex dollars for final exam time.

013. Attend at least one football game with your friends. Even if you hate football, you'll never forget the memories.

014. Be sure to watch "St. Elmo's Fire" with your closest friends before you graduate.

015. Join your student government association; they make a lot of decisions that you should be a part of.

016. If you live off campus, remember the rent and bills gotta be paid EVERY month, not just once a semester.

017. Take advantage of summer classes.

018. Go to your professor's office BEFORE you need to ask her for an extension.

019. Focus 90% of your time on solutions and only 10% of your time on problems.

020. Save at least 15% of any money you make and invest it. Compound interest is the eighth wonder of the world.

021. Be sure to meet the people who comprise your school's Division of Student Affairs. They are the most powerful and influential teachers you'll ever meet outside the classroom.

022. Rather than complain about the cafeteria food, offer the directors your mother's best recipe and ask them to prepare it, not only for you but for the whole campus!

023. Visit the health center when you are NOT sick.

024. Always carry a pocket tape recorder or a 3x5 note card with you, so you can record the things that you'll probably forget.

025. Buy postcards with your school's logo on them. Send them to your friends and family. It's easier and cheaper than writing letters.

026. The best time to use the computers is on Friday afternoons and Saturday and Sunday mornings.

027. If you see your university's president walking on campus, be sure to introduce yourself. She will be delighted to meet you. After all, you ARE paying her salary.

028. Lobby for a smoke-free campus.

029. Save all the quarters you get. Come laundry day, you'll be glad you did this.

030. Learn not only to find what you like, learn to like what you find.

031. Volunteer – not so you can "build" your resume, but so you can build your reputation.

032. Participate in the Homecoming Parade so you can bring your kids back when you're an alumnus and say, "Back when I was in college we used to......"

033. Use pictures of loved ones as book markers.

034. Never, Never, Never take No-Doz and Drink Jolt or Mellow Yellow together. The only thing you'll get is a massive brain cramp.

035. Always be a freshman.

036. Put first things first.

037. Find out who the buildings on your campus are named after and learn what they contributed to your school.

038. Never ever miss out on a road trip, no matter what the reasons.

039. Never ever miss a class. Would you pay for a house and never live in it?

040. During a rain storm, be sure to play a game of mud football with your friends.

041. Learn the history of your college.

042. Never drink alcohol when you are Hungry, Angry, Lonely, or Tired. Booze will only exacerbate these emotions.

043. If you get it on, be sure to put it on. (WEAR A CONDOM!!!)

044. Transcend political correctness and strive for human righteousness.

045. Take advantage of guest lectures. You will no doubt learn a lot from them.

046. Go to the career center during your freshman year and start a file. Don't wait until you graduate.

047. Make sure you travel to the cafeteria with at least ten people because it turns the trip into an adventure.

048. Snuggle with a friend on rainy days.

049. Be sure to read anything and everything by Tom Peters.

050. You won't get more out of college from the five or six year plan, so don't even try to kid yourself.

051. If you do choose the five year plan, you will most definitely get more of one thing—loans to pay back.

052. Don't major in minor things.

053. Get used to a diet of peanut butter, pizza, and macaroni & cheese.

054. Take a course on financial planning.

055. Be sure to attend at least one concert given by the School of Music. Your peers will impress you with what they can do.

056. When you are a senior, go back to your old dorm room and share some words of wisdom with the new freshman who now lives where you once did.

057. Learn how to set goals.

058. Take a friend out to eat once a month.

059. Know people for WHO they are rather than for what they are.

060. Never take aspirin to avoid a hangover. Aspirin will lower your blood volume and increase your blood alcohol content, thereby increasing the likelihood of a hangover.

061. Take your vitamins.

062. Read *The Seven Habits of Highly Effective People* by Stephen Covey. He is the Socrates of the 21st Century.

063. Set high standards and few limitations for yourself.

064. When in class, don't take notes. Instead, tape record the lecture. After class listen to the tape and then write notes. You get two things from this—better grades and your prof's appreciation for your attention.

065. No matter how much your friends dare you, never, ever eat the urinal blocks.

066. Don't get wasted and act obnoxious. The only thing you'll get is a hangover and fewer friends.

067. Develop a passion for learning. If you do, you will never cease to grow.

068. Make a dream list.

069. Make a joy list.

070. Contrary to popular belief, it is not the first impression that is most important. It's the 1 million and first impression that counts.Your ability to have integrity in every area of life is invaluable.

071. Remember, life is like a boomerang. Whatever you "throw" out will always come back to you.

072. Take a nap everyday.

073. If you think you're gonna "find yourself" in Seattle or Colorado, take this advice- take a good look in the bathroom mirror and get on with life. You'll save yourself a lot more than just the $157.99 bus fare.

074. Realize that if you have time to whine and complain about something, then you have the time to do something about it.

075. Read *Awaken the Giant Within* and *Unlimited Power* by Anthony Robbins at least four times in your life.

076. Use both sides of the paper no matter what your professor tells you. He has had the opportunity to walk in the woods. Our grandchildren deserve that opportunity, too.

077. Talk to alumni and ask them what it was like "back in the day".

078. Never throw away your first college ID card.

079. Always be nice to secretaries. They are the REAL gatekeepers in the world.

080. Go back to your high school and tell seniors about your college experience.

081. While in college master computers, modems, fax machines and E-mail. It is how most of us will get to work in the future.

082. Exercise every day—trust me, you'll need it.

083. Learn your college's fight song and sing it with PRIDE.

084. See your life as a movie. Write your own script, act your own part, direct your own scenes, create your own soundtrack, be your own critic and enjoy your own production.

085. Meet your advisor BEFORE you graduate!

086. Smile, it is the key that fits the lock of everybody's heart.

087. The greatest gift that you can give another person is your attention.

088. The greatest gift that you can give yourself is a little bit of your OWN attention.

089. Always carry an extra blue book in your book bag.

090. For a wild and crazy time at a party, find a large desert plant and have your friends encircle it while singing "Disco Inferno" by the Tramps.

091. Carry an apple wherever you go. When you're hungry, eat it instead of hitting a grease wagon.

092. Go camping every fall and every spring and make it a tradition.

093. Don't just prioritize your schedule, schedule your priorities.

094. If you can take the bus to class, don't drive your car, take the bus.

095. If you can walk to class, don't ride the bus, walk.

096. Manage yourself so that you can lead your life.

097. Decorate your dorm room for every holiday.
Mom is sure to have some things you can use.

098. Read the book *The Road Less Traveled*, by
Scott Peck before you graduate.

099. If you believe that discrimination exists, it will.

100. Buy your clothes at thrift stores and your furniture at yard sales. When you don't need them anymore, give them to the Salvation Army.

101. Next time you're at a hotel, take the little complimentary shoe shine brush. It will come in very handy when you need a quick shine before the formal or your first job interview.

102. Learn everything you can about how tuition and fees are set. Often your fellow students are a part of the process. Be one of those students.

103. Hold on to your books for at least one semester before you sell them back. You'll never know when they might be useful.

104. Value your self reliance more than your Social Security.

105. Look through old yearbooks to remind you that if they got through this, so can you.

106. If you see trash lying around your campus, pick it up. After all, it's YOUR front lawn for the next four years.

107. Run for a position in a student organization no matter how big or how small.

108. Vote in local elections. Local politics has a major impact on you as a student.

109. Take a speed reading course.

110. Own one very good pen.

111. Begin to plan for retirement NOW!

112. Start an IRA today.

113. If you don't know what an IRA is — find out!

114. If you put $5.55 every day into an IRA account, from the time you're 23 to the time you're 65, you will have accumulated over a half million dollars on your sixty-fifth birthday. Like #112 says — START AN IRA TODAY - no matter how old you are!

115. If life doesn't offer a game worth playing, then invent a new one.

116. Shop at the GAP at the end of each season; that's when they have the best deals.

117. Remember, a note from your mother probably won't cut it anymore.

118. Start to listen to Frank Sinatra. By age 65 you'll have all the words memorized.

119. Don't go right to graduate school after graduation. Work at least three months; you'll gain experience and money.

120. Send a birthday card to your high school sweetheart on his birthday, even if you don't date anymore.

121. If you're a freshman, draft your resume now.

122. If you're a senior and still don't have a resume, remind a freshman to do it while they're young.

123. Keep a weekly journal of your college years. Looking back on it will bring back both laughter and tears.

124. When reading your textbooks, don't highlight every single word. Instead, read a chapter first, then go back and highlight what you feel is important.

125. If you still cannot decide what to major in, then take either communications or psychology. Both are applicable in every moment of life.

126. Take one semester and study abroad. In most cases, you'll pay the same amount of tuition but gain a whole new experience.

127. Give more than take.

128. If possible, have both a major and a minor.

129. Buy a weekly planner and use it.

130. Use a desk lamp that takes a 75 watt bulb, because 60 watts doesn't give you enough light and 100 watts will burn your scalp.

131. Be a mentor.

132. Have a mentor.

133. Continually strive to improve yourself.

134. Have three phone numbers listed by your phone:
    1. Campus safety
    2. Domino's
    3. Your home phone number.

135. The best way to get ahead and stay ahead is to read ahead.

136. Buy your family college sweatshirts for Christmas.

137. Never miss the chance to watch reruns of
    The Brady Bunch or The Cosby Show.

138. Reality doesn't bite; rather our perception of reality bites.

139. Not only are you what you think you are; more so, what you think, you are.

140. Learn to sew buttons.

141. Cut your refined sugar and refined wheat intake by one half and feel the difference that it makes in your mental clarity.

142. Don't fear change, embrace it.

143. Don't be afraid to laugh so hard that milk squirts out your nose.

144. Ask questions in class.

145. Ask questions AFTER class.

146. Learn First-Aid and CPR.

147. Feel free to leave a crazy message on your answering machine. What the hell, you're in college.

148. Have a strong mind and a soft heart.

149. Remember, the Bible says, "Ask and ye shall receive," not "Bitch and make me rich."

150. Recycle.

151. Begin to plan your dream home.

152. During a test review session never ask, "Is this going to be on the exam?" Wisdom is only granted to those who find it themselves.

153. Become a student of change. It is the only thing that will remain constant.

154. Buy a walkman and at least one self-development audio program. Listen to it every morning as soon as you wake up. This is a much better way to begin the day than flipping on the news. For an excellent source of tapes, call Nightingale-Conant at: 1-800-525-9000 and request a catalog.

155. As soon as you get to college, send your mother one of those rear car window stickers that has your school's name on it. She will take great pride in mounting it on her station wagon and it will remind her of you every time she backs up the car.

156. Never underestimate the quality of state schools. By far they are the most economical and wisest choice when pursuing an undergraduate degree.

157. Apply for graduation clearance at least 2 semesters before you graduate.

158. Go in with your roommates and buy all your school supplies at an office supply store. They give you great deals when you buy in bulk.

159. Attend the annual musical.

160. Give everybody on your floor a pack of Wintergreen Lifesavers, go into the bathroom and turn the lights out. Have everybody put at least half a roll in their mouth. Then, all at once, tell everybody to chew them and look at one another. The result is a Fourth of July fireworks display. (This really works! Why? Because the sugar, when crushed, causes the oil of wintergreen to iridesce —like a firefly.)

161. Read for your own enjoyment and personal growth every day.

162. Promise yourself to live your life as a REVOLUTION and not just a process of evolution.

163. Reread your notes 30 minutes before class.

164. Rewrite your notes 30 minutes after class.

165. Trade your tunnel vision in for funnel vision.

166. Always carry more than one number 2 pencil.

167. Donate five dollars to your university's annual capital campaign.

168. Become addicted to constant and never-ending self improvement.

169. When thinking about seconds in the cafe, wait at least 20 minutes before going back. This is the amount of time it takes your brain to tell your stomach that you've had enough.

170. Never rent an apartment with electric heat unless you go to college in the south.

171. In order to purchase the product you must go to the showroom. In order to get an education, you must go to the classroom.

172. Video tape the annual MTV Video awards. Put the tape in a box so that you can rediscover it in five years.

173. Study in the library and sleep in your bed. Not vice versa.

174. When trying to add a class, don't wait until next semester. Get on the waiting list now.

175. Know the proper procedure for filing a grade appeal.

176. Eat only fruit after 8 pm.

177. Treasure your relationships,
not your possessions.

178. If you have call waiting, never, ever click over to the other line when talking to your mother. Other calls can wait, mothers shouldn't have to.

179. Wherever you live be sure to have at least four extension cords and a power strip with you.

180. Always have the power connected BEFORE you move into your apartment and have it disconnected AFTER you leave.

181. Buy a coloring book and color *outside* the lines.

182. In addition to having a "Things To Do List," have a "Things to Create List."

183. No matter your opinion of fraternities and sororities, go through rush at least once.

184. You can learn a lot from people who view the world differently than you do.

185. Rather than smoking pot, learn to meditate to achieve an altered state of consciousness.

186. Never play Twister naked unless you have of can a non-stick cooking spray.

187. Take time to admire the beauty of your campus.

188. If you ever catch on fire remember to STOP! DROP! and ROLL!

189. No matter how many credits you're carrying, work at least 15 hours a week. It will help you to manage your time and you'll get some extra spending cash.

190. The most important things in life aren't things.

191. Arrive at least five minutes early to every class.

192. Always sit in the front-center section of class. You wouldn't take the nose bleed section of a Pearl Jam concert or would you?

193. Be the last one to hang-up when you call 911.

194. Be the last one to hang-up when you call your parents.

195. At the end of each semester, write a thank you note to the professor who taught you the most.

196. Find out who David Lance Goines is and learn what his contribution is to student rights.

197. Learn to play Bocce.

198. Learn what Bocce is if you don't already know.

199. Always lock your dorm room door. Not everyone is from the small quiet town of New Cumberland, PA.

200. Always keep a spare key in your mailbox.

201. If you talk the talk, you damn well better walk the walk.

202. Never buy a new car, no matter how good the college graduate discounts are. As soon as you drive it off the lot it loses at least 25% of its value. Instead, save your money for a down payment on your first home.

203. Get the names and phone numbers of at least two people in each of your classes. They can fill you in on what you missed last Friday morning at 8 am.

204. Don't ever lend your notes out. 99% of the time you'll never see them again.

205. When you're young, try to be realistic: as you get older, become idealistic. You'll live longer.

206. If you get the chance to attend an Ivy League school don't miss your opportunities.

207. If you go to a 2-year community college don't miss your opportunities either.

208. When giving a presentation in class, give your hand out materials AFTER your presentation. This way, people will pay attention to you rather than the papers.

209. Never stop learning; knowledge doubles every 14 months.

210. Read whatever is posted on your campus bulletin board.

211. You must first get along with yourself before you can get along with others.

212. The best time to do laundry is Monday afternoons and Tuesday nights.

213. Study in the laundry room. The sound of dryers improves your concentration.

214. Even though you can't control the winds, you can always control your own sails.

215. If your school offers a rock climbing course, take it!

216. Wherever you go, no matter what the weather, always bring your own sunshine.

217. Own a Mr. Potato Head.

218. If you put garbage into your body, you'll get garbage out of it.

219. Promise a lot and give even more.

220. Don't think you've done something new by having Cheerios with beer for breakfast. It has been tried over a million times.

221. Move off campus your junior year. This will help you grow up and you'll really learn to appreciate how your parents raised you.

222. Learn how to tie a tie.

223. If you don't know how to tie a tie, have a friend who does.

224. When venturing out to a party, travel in a group no larger than five people and don't carry your beer cup.

225. Own a jeep when you're in college.

226. When calling someone be sure to use the phone number and not the fax number. That loud beep can really hurt your ears.

227. Thoughts come THROUGH people, not FROM them.

228. Something to think about . . .

STUDENTS are...
...important people on this campus.
...not cold enrollment statistics, but flesh & blood
human beings with feelings & emotions like our own.
...not people to be tolerated so that we can do our own thing.
THEY ARE OUR THING....not dependent on us.
Rather we are both interdependent upon one another.
...not an interruption of our work, but the purpose of it.
...Without students there would be no need for this institution.

229. In life, it is not what you know or who you know that counts. IT IS BOTH!

230. Never criticize or blame your parents for how you were raised. They brought you this far in the world.

231. Contrary to popular belief, the majority of college students aren't getting wasted every single weekend.

232. When you lend somebody a book, ask him for one of his books so that it can save the space for yours.

233. When you get an A+ on an exam, put it on your refrigerator. Better yet send it home to mom and ask her to put it on her fridge.

234. Attend at least one sweaty, sticky, smelly college basement party to remind you of where you don't want to end up for the rest of your life.

235. Attend at least one town council meeting in the town or city in which your school is located.

236. If a person offers to buy you a drink and you don't want it, ask him for the money instead. You'll be able to discover his true motive.

237. Write out your goals on paper every day.

238. To become politically active in issues that face Generation X get involved in Third Millennium. Call 1-212-979-2001.

239. Read *Revolution X*, by Rob Nelson and Jon Cowan. These two crusaders are an inspiration for Generation X'ers.

240. If you don't have time to iron your shirt, hang it in the bathroom before you take a shower. The steam will help to get some of the wrinkles out.

241. Make "love" an action verb.

242. Find an on-ramp to the information highway. It is the road of the future.

243. When trying to recall something your professor said, shift your eyes to the left and look to the side. This is how you can access your internal tape player.

244. Have your family visit you on family day, no matter how "embarrassed" you are. You'll cherish these memories.

245. Become a fixer, not just a fixture.

246. Write thank you notes to people who add value to life, even for the smallest of things.

247. Send a friend a care package.

248. When you receive a care package, be sure to share it.

249. When in college, take advantage of every chance to debate politics and religion. This might be your last chance to be brutally honest on these two topics.

250. Don't eat runny eggs.

251. The only real failure in life
is one not learned from.

252. Smile more than frown.

253. You don't have to hold a position in order to be a leader.

254. We were born with two ears and only one mouth. Use them in that proportion.

255. Observe the masses and do the opposite.

256. Turn your dreams into goals by placing a deadline on them.

257. Think in terms of "lifelines" rather than "deadlines".

258. Never allow your blood sugar to get low. Eat small meals every 3-4 hours.

259. Subscribe to Success magazine or ask your library to get a subscription. Call 1-800-234-7324.

260. When solving problems, dig at that roots instead of just hacking at the leaves.

261. Always use turn signals.

262. Grow antennas, not horns.

263. If you have roommates, come to an agreement that each will do her own dishes. This will avoid over 75% of your fights.

264. For a nourishing and inexpensive snack, mix 2 cups raisins and 1 cup peanuts with 1/2 cup chocolate chips.

265. Eat fresh fruit.

266. Eat dried fruit.

267. Consider becoming a vegetarian.

268. Resist the urge to steal street signs. After four years of accumulating them, you won't know what the hell to do with them.

269. Have a huge crush on somebody.

270. ALWAYS, ALWAYS take your own roll of toilet paper.

271. Sit down and close your eyes for at least 10 minutes every day. (But not in class!)

272. The rules have changed. True power is held by the person who possesses the largest bookshelf, not gun cabinet or wallet.

273. If you want to get your security deposit back, be sure to clean your apartment once a month.

274. Even if you are not "religious," develop your own sense of spirituality.

275. If you have a vision, do something with it.

276. The parking spaces in front of bars are for the designated drivers, not the drinkers.

277. Become addicted to hugs not drugs.

278. Don't reinvent the wheel, just realign it.

279. It is no longer the Information Age, it is the Innovation Age.

280. Your college education has a very, very short shelf life. Be sure to commit yourself to life long learning.

281. Instead of stewing, start doing.

282. Read the Wall Street Journal every Monday.

283. IQ stands for Imagination Quotient not intelligence quotient.

284. Learn what The People's Network is. It will be the MTV of tomorrow's top achievers.

285. If you wanna win in the game of life, you gotta have three things: One, a good game plan; two, a good coach; and three, a good team.

286. Create your own reality.

287. No matter your opinion of money, read the book <u>Think and Grow Rich</u>, by Napoleon Hill. This book will change the way you think about money.

288. Life is meant to be enjoyed,
not endured.

289. To get a better understanding of how Economics really work, read *Unlimited Wealth* by Paul Zane Pilzer.

290. Write a thank you letter to Rosa Parks.

291. Visit the grave of JFK.

292. Watch out for the wizzer bikes!

293. Watch the movie <u>Gandhi</u>.

294. Read the autobiography of Malcolm X.

295. Own a good camera and take lots of pictures.

296. Don't pass judgment on yourself, others, or your own ideas.

297. Action conquers fear.

298. Borrow other people's ideas and apply them to yourself.

299. Don't be just a dreamer, be a doer.

300. Realize the difference between human doing and human being.

301. Experience the difference between human doing and human being.

302. Whenever you feel depressed, go to the closest airport and watch people reunite.

303. Listen to your intuition. It will tell you everything you need to know.

304. Develop a healthy attitude towards taking risks.

305. Innovate rather than emulate.

306. Enroll in the school of hard knocks—No matter what the cost of tuition.

307. When climbing the ladder of success, be sure that it is leaning against the right wall.

308. Turn fear into desire.

309. View your notebooks as an artist would view her canvas.

310. In order to succeed you must fail, so that you know what not to do the next time.

311. Our mind is like a parachute. It only works if it is open.

312. The people who oppose your ideas the most, are those who represent the establishment that your ideas will upset.

313. The prophet has never been accepted in his home land.

314. Keep your peace of mind as your number one value.

315. Buy a new toothbrush every three months.

316. Never let your persistence and passion turn into stubbornness and ignorance.

317. Become a student of Jim Rohn, Brian Tracy, Les Brown and Dennis Waitley. The knowledge & wisdom that they convey is truly empowering and life changing.

318. Make a lot of mistakes, but don't make too much of them.

319. Rather than hitting the bottle after a rough week of exams, hit a punching bag.

320. Listen to "Canon in D", by Pachelbel, whenever you have difficulty concentrating.

321. Build your reputation by helping other people build theirs.

322. Turn your strongest weakness into your greatest strength.

323. Build a better you.

324. Nourish your body with good food.

325. Nourish your mind with good books.

326. Nourish your soul with good friends.

327. Always say to yourself, "If it is to be, it is up to me."

328. Smiles are free, so don't save them.

329. Think in cans, not cannots.

330. Martin Luther King Jr. had a dream. Do you?

331. There are only three days of the week: yesterday, tomorrow, and most importantly, today.

332. Whenever there is a recession, just decide not to participate in it.

333. Get an American Express Card as soon as you graduate. It will help you establish good credit and encourage you to pay your balance in-full every month. The number is 1-800-THE-CARD.

334. Be careful of where you place your attention. You may be paying more than you have to.

335. In order to hit home runs, you gotta step up to the plate and take a swing.

336. Don't compete, rather create cooperation.

337. Run to meet the future or it's going to run you down.

338. If you don't know where you are going, you'll probably end up somewhere else.

339. If you see someone having a seizure, don't place anything in his mouth, regardless of what your mother told you.

340. Look at rainy days as being romantic rather than being gloomy.

341. Live every moment as if it were impossible for you to fail.

342. Learn how to operate a fire extinguisher. (Don't practice with the ones in your dorm. Someone might need them in order to save YOUR life someday.)

343. If you plan to attend grad school, choose a school in the same state as your undergrad school. This way, after your first two years, you can declare residency and save a bundle on out-of-state tuition.

344. Live for everyday, not just the weekends.

345. Watch a farmer plow his field.

346. It is true that life is like a box of chocolates, but contrary to Forrest Gump's mother, you DO know what you're gonna get. You can always tell which ones have the yummy caramel and nuts and which ones have that gooey cream that nobody likes. Just like chocolates, you gotta look closely at what you might pick up in life.

347. It is more important to have an accurate compass than a detailed map.

348. Community service is the rent we pay for the privilege of living in this world.

349. Support Public Broadcasting.

350. Replace the status quo of TGIF with TGIT-Thank God It's Today.

351. Just because something is a tradition doesn't make it right.

352. All the knowledge in the world is found within you.

353. The only way to solve problems is to solve them.

354. Self-discipline means self-caring.

355. Life is a series of problems.
Are we going to whine about them or
are we going to do something about them?

356. The difference between a healthy personality and a
healthy character is that a healthy personality means
getting along with others and a healthy character
means getting along with yourself.

357. Improve your personality and nurture your character.

358. Anonymous was a woman!

359. The only people in this world who don't have problems "reside" in graveyards.

360. The greatest risk that we will ever take is to grow up.

361. For some incredibly great ideas on how to make a difference in this world read *What Can I Do to Make a Difference?* by Richard Zimmerman.

362. We tend to believe what the people around us believe.

363. Discover new friends.

364. You cannot be a source of strength unless you nurture your own strength.

365. True courage is not the absence of fear; rather it is the taking of action in spite of the fear.

366. Illuminate your world rather than putting blinders around it.

367. Every gigantic oak tree started out as a tiny acorn.

368. Rediscover old friends.

369. Reflect upon yesterday, dream about tomorrow, live for today and cherish this moment.

370. Always respect those who are absent if you want to retain the respect of those who are present.

371. Stay committed to your commitments.

372. Lower your socks, not your standards.

373. In your thirst for knowledge, be sure not to drown in all the information.

374.

Normal is BORING.

375. Those who say it cannot be done should get the hell out of the way of those who are doing it.

376. Even the poorest of people in the world are creditworthy.

377. If you have a short range view, be sure to have a long range perspective.

378. Rather than just asking "how" and "when." Ask "what" and "why".

379. Choose to see your world anew.

380. To get a better feel for the future, read *The Third Wave* by Alvin Toffler. This book is THE handbook for the future.

381. A leader is a person you will follow to a place you wouldn't go by yourself.

382. Solving problems gives meaning to our lives.

383. Learn all you can about Jimmy Carter. After all he is the only man ever to have used the U.S. presidency as a stepping-stone to even greater service.

384. You'll see it, only if you believe it first.

385. Without a sense of caring, there can be no sense of community.

386. The quickest way to kill the human spirit is to allow it to do half-ass work.

387. You can and should shape your own future. If you don't, someone else surely will.

388. Savor anticipation. It is one of the greatest pleasures that life has to offer.

389. None of us are bigger than life itself.

390. Learn from these not-so-famous last words...

"The phonograph is not of any commercial value."
-Thomas Edison, 1880.

"Sensible and responsible women do not want
to vote." *-Grover Cleveland, 1905.*

"Babe Ruth made a big mistake when he gave up
pitching."*-Tris Speaker, 1921.*

"Who the hell wants to hear actors talk?"
-Harry Warner, Warner Brothers Pictures, 1927.

"There is no reason for anybody to have a computer
in their home." *-Ken Olsen, president of Digital Equipment Corporation, 1977.*

391. Learn what paradigms are so that you can pioneer them.

392. You can and should shape your own attitude. If you don't, someone else surely will.

393. Keep trying in trying times.

394. Your future is where your greatest leverage lies.

395. Always finish what you start no matter how big or how small the project might be.

396. The joy of life is finding rainbows in thunderstorms.

397. See the commonality of
diversity so that you may see
the diversity of commonality.

398. Become a sucker for an optimist.

399. There is no such thing as a free lunch. (Unless you go to Denny's on your birthday!)

400. One of the greatest tools in the universe is our imagination.

401. We were not put on this earth to fail, we are all here to succeed.

402. Luck is the residue of hard work.

403. Success in life doesn't come from holding a good hand. It comes from playing a good one well.

404. Your greatest asset is your brain-USE IT.

405. Knowledge has no value unless it is implemented.

406. The person who cannot follow a leader intelligently can not become an intelligent leader.

407. Accountability breeds responsibility.

408. Either we control our desires or they control us.

409. Look at college this way:
You are a customer. The college
is the company that sells you,
the customer, a product, which
is your education.

The college hires salesmen, the faculty, to sell you the product. In other words, ALWAYS DEMAND A QUALITY EDUCATION!

410. More people in America die as a result of overeating than from hunger.

411. In the battle of "Mind vs. Mattress," never let the mattress win.

412. Succeed at results.

413. Shit doesn't "just" happen. People make shit happen.

414. No free society should ever be afraid of words.

415. We only live life once, but if we live it right, one time is all we'll need.

416. In life you can choose to be a thermostat or a themometer. A thermostat influences its environment, whereas a thermometer is influenced BY its' environment. Which are you???

417. Resist the urge to do more. Do less better.

418. Most of the shadows in our lives are caused by standing in our own sunshine.

419. We tend to start out speaking as we think, but end up thinking as we speak.

420. One of the heaviest things that you'll ever let go of is your own ego.

421. The difference between wise people and fools is in their choice of tools.

422. The secret to a beautiful painting is knowing what NOT to put on canvas. Likewise, the secret to a beautiful life is knowing what NOT to put in it.

423. Over commitment is one of the greatest ways to dilute our effectiveness.

424. No one can make you feel inferior without your own consent.

425. An expert is merely a person who is 100 miles away from home.

426. Overcome to become.

427. Our thoughts move faster than our feelings.

428. Don't accept the status quo-
CHALLENGE IT.

429. Today is a day which we need not dream, only realize.

430. There is no better feeling on this earth than to give a little of yourself to brighten another person's day.

431. If you wanna get anywhere in this world, you gotta have a road map. LEARN TO SET GOALS! For a great tool read *What Are Your Goals?* by Gary Ryan Blair.

432. Plans are worthless, but planning is invaluable.

433. Believe in others when they have lost faith in themselves.

434. Leaders are neither made nor born. Rather they are remade and reborn through the process of learning from experience.

435. Whenever learning a new skill or topic, act as if you are already an expert. No doubt you'll become one.

436. Our thoughts are the ONLY thing in this world that we can control. Take advantage of this.

437. Don't just learn information, learn skills.

438. All experiences will do something for you or some thing to you. The choice is yours.

439. Cultivate the habit of doing more than you are paid or expected to do.

440. See your stumbling blocks as stepping stones.

441. The best way to predict your future is to create it.

442. Live in your imagination more than your memory.

443. Follow your goodness.

444. Share your kindness.

445. Encourage laughter.

446. Discover miracles.

447. Honor the wonderful person you continue to become.

448. Unity is not sameness; rather it is synergistic interdependence.

449. Listen to National Public Radio.

450. Rather than condemn another person's weakness, compliment it with one of your strengths.

451. Never tear down anything, unless you are prepared to put something better in its place.

452. It is okay to have butterflies in your stomach, just make sure that they are flying in formation.

453. Turn lemons into lemonade.

454. DO IT NOW!!!

455. Your circumstances
don't define you;
rather they reveal you.

456. Whenever someone says, "You can't do it,"
say, "Maybe YOU can't, but I can!"

457. Don't eat things with a face.

458. If you give an ignorant person one million dollars,
they're gonna blow it. If you take a million dollars
away from an educated person they will earn it back.

459. Don't just add years to your life; rather add life
to your years.

460. Join the World Future Society. By the year 2020 it will have more clout than the NRA & the AARP combined, because it only has one "special interest" in mind- our future.
Call 1-800-989-8274 for a membership kit.

461. When buying anything be sure to look beyond the price so that you can see the value.

462. Request songs on your school's radio station.

463. To learn the secret of how to be financially independent by age 30, read *The Richest Man in Babylon* by George Clason.

464. Read *As A Man Thinketh* before you die.

465. Learn how to network. It is one of the key life skills.

466. Ignore other people's ignorance so that you may discover your own wisdom.

467. In life you can either choose to be a bug or a windshield.

468. If you don't get the last one; In life you can be the lawn or the lawnmower. Don't let your ass become the grass!

469. Don't go through life, GROW through life!

470. To learn how to network, read anything and everything by Harvey Mackay.

471. Get an E-mail address now! For a great on-line service call America Online at 1-800-827-6364.

472. As my mother says, "Don't wait for the calendar to tell you. Make everyday a 'Hallmark' day."

473. Never eat in a restaurant that doesn't have windows.

474. The U.S. legal system is not perfect, but it is the best. And it is the best because it is not perfect.

475. Volunteer against illiteracy . The only degree you need is a degree of caring. Call 1-800-228-8813.

476. If you are ever lacking faith in America, visit Independence Hall in Philadelphia, PA. You will regain a whole new sense of what our country is all about.

477. Invite your brothers & sisters to your school on sibling weekend. THEY MISS YOU.

478. Own one nice navy blue suit.

479. Don't kiss people who smoke. Would you lick an ashtray?

480. Develop an attitude of gratitude.

481. If you lend a friend money be sure to have him sign an IOU and charge him interest for the loan. This way you won't lose your money or your friendship.

482. Learn how to bake good bread.

483. Never throw away your ATM receipts. Keep them in a small box and every two weeks enter the transactions in your checkbook.

484. Invite your friends who cannot travel home to your house for the holidays. It will mean a lot to them.

485. Nowadays, even Pinnochio needs to wonder if his date has termites. So should you. It's a little bug called AIDS.

486. Always be prepared for that surprise Sunday morning visit that your parents are bound to make. (This means don't go out and get trashed on Saturday night.)

487. Whenever you say good-bye to your parents, hug them and say "I love you".

488. Life is short, cherish it.

489. Always have a copy of Reader's Digest in your bathroom. It is the world's mostly widely read magazine. For a subscription call: 1-800-723-1241.

490. Remember this inevitable fact of college life:
On move-in day the temperature will be in the 90's
with 97% humidity. Your room will be on the ninth
floor and the elevator will break down. Be prepared,
be patient.

491. Patronize the local shops and restaurants in the town
in which your school is located. Many of the owners
are likely to be alumni. Besides, students have a huge
impact on the local economy, by helping them you
are helping yourself!

492. Write a thank you letter to the high school teacher you could not stand now that you are grateful for what he taught you. Do the same thing for that one college teacher in ten years.

493. Be sure to follow the career of your high school's star athlete. After all, he may become the quarterback for the Dallas Cowboys.

494. Be sure to follow the career of your high school's class valedictorian. After all, she may become America's next President.

495. Live simply so that others
can simply live.

496. Write for your school paper. The pen is truly mightier than the sword.

497. The grass on the other side of the fence is whatever color <u>YOU</u> make it.

498. When it absolutely, positively has to be there overnight - Use Federal Express. Call 1-800-238-5355.

499. Learn the story of Fred Smith. He's the guy who created FED EX.

500. Consider starting your own business, but before you do read *The E-Myth* by Michael Gerber. He is an ordinary man with extraordinary ideas.

501. Learn the story of Wayne Huizenga. He is the man who created Blockbuster Video.

502. Drink Snapple.

503. Watch Oprah, Larry King Live, CNN and QVC.

504. Keep in mind that you don't have to graduate magna cum laude in order for your school to dedicate a wing of the library in your honor- Just ask David Letterman.

505. Visit Disney World.

506. Dream impossible dreams and live an enchanted life.

507. Answer this question: What one great thing would you dare to do if you knew that you could not fail? What are you waiting for??

One final thought...

Take time to work; it is the price of success.

Take time to think; it is the source of power.

Take time to play; it is the secret of perpetual youth.

Take time to read; it is the foundation of wisdom.

Take time to be friendly; it is the road to happiness.

Take time to love and be loved; it is the privilege of the gods.

Take time to share; life is too short to be selfish.

Take time to laugh; laughter is the music of the soul.

                                    -Irish Prayer, author unknown

About The Author

Anthony D'Angelo is nationally known as the **Obi-Wan Kenobi** of the personal development field. He is the founder and executive director of **EmPower X!, Inc.**, a non-profit educational organization dedicated to empowering young adults aged 18-28. Through EmPower X! Mr. D'Angelo has introduced hundreds of thousands of young adults to the ideas, concepts and educational resources of the world's leading personal development experts- the Yodas.

At the early age of 23, armed only with a VISA Card, a supportive family and an inspiring vision *To Help Take Higher Education Deeper* he created EmPower X!. Within two years he built a nationally recognized non-profit personal leadership organization for young adults, which is privileged to serve a client roster that reads like the Fortune 500 List of Higher Education, including institutions such as MIT, The University of Pennsylvania and Princeton University. Both Mr. D'Angelo and EmPower X! have been featured on several national media outlets including CNN Interactive, CNNFN and SPIN Magazine. In addition to his work with EmPower X! he serves as a consultant to businesses, organizations and institutions of Higher Education in the United States and abroad. Mr. D'Angelo is currently working on his second book entitled, *Most People Die When They're 23, But They're Not Buried Until They're 70!: A Personal Leadership Handbook and Resource Guide.*

Tony is a native of New Cumberland, Pennsylvania and graduate of Cedar Cliff High School and West Chester University. He now lives in the small Victorian town of Lambertville, New Jersey and will marry his college sweetheart, Christine Randazzese, in July of 1998. He thanks you for reading this book & looks forward to meeting you in person.

EmPower X!, Inc.
Helping You Take Higher Education Deeper™

The mission of EmPower X! is to Awaken, Enliven, Inspire and Empower young adults between the ages of 18-28 to significantly enhance their quality of life in order to achieve & fulfill worthwhile purposes in this world. We meet this noble challenge in two ways. First we help young adults to discover, nurture and apply their own Personal Leadership. Secondly we introduce them to the ideas, concepts and educational resources of the world's foremost Personal Leadership experts. This synergistic approach allows us to help young adults become more by supporting the never ending search for the best within themselves.

We all are X's.
For some people, that X means being an unknown.
For a few, like you, that means being a **multiplication factor**.
You are different. You are a leader. You make things happen.
While most of your peers are getting degrees you are getting an education.
We help people like you take higher education deeper.

Life is short. You have dreams.
We realize this and make it our mission to help you achieve those dreams.
We are dream architects. Some people design buildings.
We help people like you design your life.
See you on your campus soon.